MW01534116

Mornings by
The River

Poems in the order
of things

Kathleen E. Fearing, Ed.D

Storyteller Productions
© 2012
All Rights Reserved.

Dedication
This work is dedicated to all those who watch,
who see things about them and wonder;
and especially
to the fabulous members
of my writers' group.

Table of Contents

Mornings by the River

Poems in the Order
of Things

"How could drops of water know themselves to be a river? Yet the river flows on."
(Antoine de Saint-Exupery)

Mornings by the River

A New Day

Yesterday
thunder shook me from
my secluded dream,
the earth shuddered…then,
clouds,
so full of themselves,
unleashed
rain's indifferent hand,
my hidden garden razed in its wake.

Today,
as the penitent lover asks forgiveness,
a meek wind blow-dries
bent, weeping pansies,
a touch of peach
brims the parting clouds…and,
discovering a new horizon
I scrape off the rain
and go on.

Alternate Views

The smoke and mirrors
I clothe myself with during the day
for the world to judge me by,
hang on a hook behind my closet door,
set aside until tomorrow
when I'll take them up again…
Now, my bed welcomes me
without judgment,
I feel my thighs,
cupboards for yesterday's cupcakes,
thinking how long they've walked with me,
it doesn't matter
here, I feel my breasts,
happy children escaped from school,
and my belly's stretched skin,
evidence of my babies for the world to see,
that world that tells me
what and who to be,
but, here,
I am
me.

Anonymous Days

Yesterday's painful harvest
is swallowed then re-chewed
each night in dreams,
like a never-ending cow's cud,
as if doing so will make it palatable,
instead of indigestible wreckage.
The mind's eye considers
life's ironies:
the cereal in my morning bowl
floats on milk,
then drowns beneath it;
the child who once nuzzled
at my breast, contented,
becomes a stranger;
a dream's light,
refracted,
reveals a path
different from the one planned…still,
the days come,
come one after the other, and
each day's survival must be celebrated—
must be written in bursts of red
on the distant pages of sunset.

Another Road

You were three when
you first ran from me
down the road, where
I chased you—your baby curls,
like downy wings,
flying in the wind—afraid
you would be lost, or
killed by a car,
wondering what you ran toward,
or from.
And today, when
you said no,
you couldn't help with
my book, so many other
things to do,
my inner eye glimpsed the baby girl,
curls flying.

Ashes

Withered fingers
lie still, cold,
though once they
clapped at recitals,
unknotted strands of summer hair,
held my world together…

until, something happened
I could not know or define,
but felt it
in the air around you,
withering your soul
snatching at your fragile sanity.

Now, ashes tremble,
rush into the death storm
to find what we know
is waiting, yet shun,
like a lost love we
can not forgive.

Attachment

A lone fiber,
dipped in dew and morning,
stretches from my roof
to the young sapling out my window.
A spider left it—
   a slender thought
   spanning the void—
attaching me
to her tree, and,
like Alice after the rabbit,
I trace her steps
down the tenuous path to
endless possibilities.

Autumn

Autumn,
  my two-faced friend,
comes at me all smiles and warm winds
spreading sweet perfumes of sugar maples
through musky, earthy-scented woods –
  my great euphoria.

Our friendship stretches thin when
only lost, lethargic bees remain and
squirrels chase each other's shadows in neurotic
circles –
  their small mouths bulged to
  nearly bursting with mid-winter meals –
stopping here and there to secrete acorns –
  not just one or two,
  but dozens in my fertile flower beds, or
  scattered pattern-less about my lawn –
one, forgotten underneath my back steps, takes
hold:
  a tree to bloom in spring.

Sweet autumn's friendly face morphs to a
chilling scowl when wind –
  no longer whispering her soft, warm
  southern drawl –
becomes a cold stampede cascading down from
flat Canadian plains,
tears maize and crimson leaves from their
summer mother's arms,

blows them about my head like scattered
pieces of sun
creating multi-colored blizzards –
> gathered in rambunctious piles, produce
> a leafy blanket for woods to winter
> dream beneath –
but all too soon turn brown when frosty
nights bite their backs and raw,
cold rain transforms them to a thick
brown sludge that
chokes my grass.

Ah…although each year at summer's end again
I plead,
> 'tis no use…
another autumn thumbs its nose to friendship,
then turns its gray face northward
beckoning my old nemesis, winter,
stealing another pound of flesh.

Being Alive

Some days,
not in the morning, but
late afternoon, when thoughts
pile up, when memories
slither down the back of my neck,
like cold rain off the brim
of my hat,
to rearrange
themselves in my stomach's pit,
it's then that being-alive tears try their
damnedest to escape
and haunt my soul;
and, sometimes, not
always, but sometimes they do, until
I push them back, reminding
myself that everyone treads in
a shadowed well of those
same tears, and,
if we let them have their way,
the world
would drown
in yesterday.

Mornings by the River

"When the river is deepest it makes the least noise."
(Proverb, anonymous)

Mornings by the River

Bird Houses

We planted seven trees yesterday.
Out my kitchen window
I watch—anxious,
like a new mother watches her child
on an unfamiliar playground.
Warm rain falls
rooting each to its spot,
and, one by one, they realize
their calling,
make ready for spring
and birds, who do not search
for meaning,
who need nothing but
a slender branch
to call home.

Blind

I know fog is
a test,
making us search
its murky curtain,
like a child strains to look
through a crowd to see a parade.

My neighbor's house hovers in its gray veil,
I feel it, wet, shivering…
and, peering through
half-open blinds,
hold my breath,
wondering what that dark shape is…

Change

The clouds have changed
direction today—
       north to south instead of
       west to east—
and I think about
directions and change—
       is it easier for clouds
       than for people? and,
       what might have happened to me
       if I had not?
Still, clouds adjust and
grow and cry turbulent tears
and rebuild, perhaps
flowing in a different
direction,
but going on,
giving in to inescapable, possibly
frightening alteration—
       what if I am never
       like I was…what if I become lost—
yet, clouds eternally
remake themselves into what
they need to be.

Choices

Bacon in the soup
or beef?
Hair long
or short?
Be as man's church dictates
or follow my heart?
Smile and ignore stupidity
or speak my mind?
Seek truths disguised in
fluid clouds
pulled and pushed against
their will
or follow the path
chosen?
I know
what I must do.

Communication

Crows search for breakfast in
dew-soaked grass,
rebellion carved in every caw.
I edge toward my window—
        like cupping my ear toward muffled
        voices from another room,
        trying to comprehend.

In unison, the crows explode upward,
settle on phone lines,
spaced just so,
sway back and forth to keep their balance, and,
sensing the buzz beneath their claws,
lean down, straining to know—
        yin and yang,
        endlessly circling.

Daffodils

Ice conquers fragile,
paper-thin skins
raw winter leaves shrunken,
lifeless,
though once they bloomed,
fearless,
as sweet April rain pulsed
through fluttering, yellow heads.

Buried far beneath December's
killing cold,
spring's fecund promise whispers 'courage', and
stirs hungry hearts
from dormant shells,
   open…
   vulnerable…
   alive!

Days Gone

Pencil lines dart
through squares on my calendar
southwest to northeast
the days of my life
gone killed
by a pencil
a stroke of my hand
another page turned
days forever lost
crossed out
by gray pencil lines
careless of
what happened there
or failed to.

Dreams

Flashes of emotion
burst through the dense
undergrowth of my sleep,
then leave just as quickly…
a son's smile,
an old boss' frown,
frustration about
something
I could not put
my finger on, but
knew it for what it was,
a failure somewhere
in my past,
one that stuck like telltale mud
on Sunday shoes,
one that loops back around
nightly—a relentless
mosquito whispering in
my sleeping ear,
        'I'm back'

Enigmatic River

Enigmatic river,
broad yet narrow,
springtime rain-swelled river,
you escape your earthen banks
creating necessary havoc,
nourishing the once-dry land,
eternally meandering,
adjusting boundaries at your whim,
leaves ride your back for free
sightseeing along the way to nowhere;
thoughtful river–
nature's mirror to the sky–
how is it you bear without complaint
heavy motorboats, canoes and kayaks
on your back, tolerate fishers fishing
throwing hooks into your secret places?
merciless river, dammed by drowning
trees reaching up for help,
are they but curiosities as
your swift waters persist southward
toward their ancient home?
yet still I see you here…
though not a tree,
your branches reach into the land,
strange birds and alligators live
along your bayous,
hungry fish jump high to catch fat bugs
flying in dizzy swarms
exposed by shafts of sunlight on your head;

weather-beaten houses perch precariously by
your side watching helpless as you scrape
away the land beneath them,
twisting neatly into ox-bows where
there are no oxen;
born in black storm clouds and hidden springs,
you flow down mountain sides
creating canyons deeper
than earth's highest peaks;
ripples on your skin morph to tiny whirlpools
then become white water, tumbling,
cursing jagged rocks just beneath your
surface 'til you widen with a
placid grin, that self-assured lover's smile,
fooling everyone
but you.

Fate-
A sonnet

I caught a glimpse of fate while flying high,
Too far away to grasp, to draw it near,
And though its calling filled the evening sky,
My ears had turned inside and could not hear.

A youthful indecision hindered love,
Thereafter stealing sunshine from my eyes,
No more its brightness filtered from above,
No more sweet laughter echoed in my sighs.

But fate did not desert me after all,
Though once I did but think that all was lost,
For somewhere in the night you heard my call,
There I prepared to go despite the cost.

My heart cannot decide what's right or wrong,
But opens only to your heartfelt song.

Mornings by the River

"What makes a river so restful to people is that it doesn't have any doubt – it is sure to get where it is going, and it doesn't want to go anywhere else."
(Hal Boyle)

Mornings by the River

Fear

How do we learn
to dread
what has not happened,
and might never?
Anxious, we hold our step,
hesitate,
peer into the frozen sky,
searching…for what?
Can one love with half a heart?

Hesitant

The words are there, but,
if I open myself
like a forbidden book,
tear at the eggshell pages of
my insides,
let the tears escape,
will I be able to see
tomorrow?

House For Rent

The back porch dips westerly now,
its fulcrum—doomed by gravity,
        slow spring rains, termites—
waits for repair
and new tenants.

Sunflowers—once reflected in
        curtain-draped windows,
        heads bobbing 'round a cracked
        foundation—
over time, surrendered to
transient feet.

The old house sat, people-less,
sounds of doors slamming—
        a child's sobbing nightmare,
        arguments about what was not—
lingering deep within its timbers.

Now the repairman labors, soothing injury done
by some who didn't bother about
the hurt left behind—
        windows, like old cracked bones unable
        to knit—
they'd moved on.

Invisible Strings

The bushes just off
my back porch
are jam-packed with cardinals
making ready for spring…
red flashes flit
branch to branch,
swaying like live
Christmas tree ornaments, and
with unseen strings
they tug at me…until,
I am one of them,
allowed, for a brief moment,
to share in their restless pursuit
of life's impossible ending.

It Was the Forget-Me-Nots

It was the forget-me-nots,
pressed between saffron pages,
still faintly blue,
scarred, creased
where someone held them too tightly…
loose ends of yesterday's summer
sliced from their roots,
bound with frayed, pink ribbon,
petals wide, like pinwheels frozen
in a dream unfulfilled…

It was the forget-me-nots
picked again in haste,
as a girl running toward love
fails to look,
stumbles over rocks she
knew were there,
forgetting how painful rocks and
flowers can be.

Lady in Waiting

She sits,
almost unnoticeable,
but I see her there,
in the tree outside my window,
so steady in the midst of the storm,
watching what happens around her—
muted colors blending with
browns and golds of Fall…
patient for opportunity,
and a time
when the day is not so cold,
and the sun warms her heart again.

Laundry, etc.

Summer,
laundry day,
stick figure people hung out to dry,
sheets slapped by pine-fresh wind
hold a prickly-green scent
that lingers through my nighttime
out-of-doors dreams.

Rainy days,
laundry drip-dries
on a line Mummy stretches
end-to-end across the kitchen.
It sags from diapers,
Dad's work shirts and socks,
creates an indoor tropical front,
a wet booby-trap for the unmindful.

Then, a gas dryer found a spot in the kitchen,
my sheets were cooked 'til done,
something called Snuggle made them smell
chemical, foreign, killing my
out-of-doors dreams.

Never

The hefty perfume
of springtime laurels
weighs down the air
I breathe…
a magician's potion, it
drives the bees to mayhem,
gorging on the life they sense
in the dust clinging,
like a lover, to golden legs;
and woven in their hums,
laced throughout never-ending motion,
I hear:
            never give up -
            never give up -
            never…

Night Vision

Lightning rips a hole in the darkness
and all around me,
like lost angels,
cottonwood seeds drift
in the sizzling air.
My hands reach out to grab them,
the fleet tufts dance,
slip away,
like giddy children playing
hide'n'seek,
twirl helpless in hot prairie dust,
affix themselves to
my hair,
to worn, traveled jeans,
seeking that place of rapture among
their sisters.
Some let go of their wind song,
fall softly to the pavement,
their promise
crushed by passing cars
racing on to find the cottonwood trees.

Not Yet

A tree in winter
holds fast to its children—
>buds not yet allowed
>to open,
>not yet ready
>to be tugged at by tempestuous wind,
>endure pelting rain—

but today,
when the sun brushed
tight-lipped seams,
they burned
with adolescent promise of things
unknown, impatient
to open their hearts—
>vulnerable to life.

Now

One small breath
I'm caught in the heat of you
One light touch
I'm lost in the feel of you
The strength of your arm
Weakens me
The scent of your sweat
Washes over me
I crawl inside you
Wanting nothing more
Needing everything
Devouring all

OCD

An anxious little bug
dances inside me,
twitches at the thought of
something left undone,
a place of 'rest'
is its own foreign country,
'doing' is its
only comfort,
tying loose ends,
checking to see
if what's done is right,
checking ten, twenty times,
and then,
        once more—once more….

Mornings by the River

" If my ship sails from sight, it
doesn't mean my journey ends, it simply
means the river bends."
(John Enoch Powell)

Mornings by the River

One More

One more winter
melts away
its suffering chill
leaves my bones
one season
older
one more spring
erupts beneath
my feet
its soft elastic boundaries
fling me back to when
there were no bad dreams
no regretted words
only the un-trod
road ahead
to what
might be.

Open Blinds

I open the blinds,
halfway, at first—
vivid light startles me—
then, wide…all the way…all the way,
'til the slender smile of sun,
like a mother's forgiving touch, caresses
old creases and frowns—roadmaps
of hurt and desire…

I am the hibernating
bear gulping her first breath in spring,
I fill my lungs—
      stunted
      by the winter of another time—
to near bursting, then,
exhale years of turmoil
trapped inside my aching self.

Perceptions

And the grounds became fertile again
and the earth warmed
and moved toward the sun,
but some things,
some one,
moves further away,
grasping at clouded perceptions
of me,
not letting go,
never letting go…
can I dig the knife in
any deeper,
would it matter to someone
who can't
hear my cries?

Poets

I read
words of poets
in magazines
in books I've bought
and wonder at their courage
exposing hideous scar tissue
words covered with blood tears
and I am afraid that
if I did the same
it might kill me
or at the very least
like Sylvia
lock me in a room
from where I could not escape
yet the words
beckon me
slip from my pen
like strands of just-washed hair
in their
uncontrollable beauty.

Proof of Life

Are we but shadows
to come or go
at the whim of light?
Do we exist in midnight's
murky void?
Is there no way to know?
Swaying in the hammock of
unconsciousness,
are we still there,
full of breath and blood, or,
lost in the stillness of somewhere,
do we teeter on the knife-edge of being?
Does a thought travel
forever into darkness
if no one is there to receive it?
Do I exist without
you?
My shadow bends
toward your gravity.

Shadows

A buzzard's shadow drifts
across my lawn,

a soundless warrior
stalking prey,

silence grows
in its wake, and

I pull away,
hidden, safe,

hold my breath,
trembling

from a fear
I can't define.

Shepherd

The farm
down the street
has a new crop of lambs
spring babies
so small
with long busy tails
knobby wool coats
some white
others chocolate brown
while a man
wearing a tattered brown coat
a scruffy three or four day beard
in rubber boots to mid calf
stands among them
a new born lamb in his arms
his demeanor content
as he strokes the lamb's head
saying something I cannot hear.

Standing Watch

Out the back door
Wild flowers bend toward the sun
Lean against tall grass
Not mown for some time now
You used to do that
One of your favorite things
You'd say
Not mine
I would watch you circle the house
Again and again
Sweat on your forever brow
Grass stains on large, gentle hands
That waved to me
As I stood watching.

Stop Over

Large, gray geese,
outlined against November
overcast, call out,
hell-bent on their journey…
the old bull eyes
a stubbed patch of ground,
remains of a once bright
yellow harvest…
exhausted, they settle in
a great whoosh of wings and squawks,
peck and stab at frosty ground,
gleaning what
they can; tired, but not yet done,
they peck once more, ruffle and
settle weary wings,
stroke each other's crooked necks,
mutter a quiet goodnight, 'til
morning erupts in cold sparks, and
again they scan the skies
to find a sign, a way,
and I,
caught up in their aching storm,
turn from my window, teary.

Mornings by the River

" Even the upper end of the river
believes in the ocean."
(William Stafford)

Mornings by the River

Strings

One led from
me to the post
at the end of my porch,
another to the fiddles and banjos
floating around
my neighbor's radio,
a multitude
connected me to
the whirling cloud of bugs,
drawn by their own
strings to my
newly bloomed laurel;
one other string,
frayed,
alternately slackened
or taut,
pulled me toward you—
        the only one I'm afraid
        to cut.

Summer Vacation/Dream

Vacation: a curious word.
I have no place to vacate,
except reality,
to bike thru Italy's rolling amber hills,
run boiling rapids of the muddy Colorado,
summit icy mountain peaks…or not.
It all makes me tired. Instead,
I dream of summers long passed, and,
once again warm pond water gushes
up my nose,
catches me off guard, and
I laugh, choking on the pungent liquid,
my small body rolls down Granny's
fresh cut lawn,
cedar shingles on the south side of the house
bake in the sun's oven,
pink and purple pansy heads
bob in midday breezes,
friend's voices call 'my gools, one, two, three,
        come find me, come find me…'
somewhere in a lost summer.

Sun in the Afternoon

Dobs of sun
find my afternoon resting place,
track across my thigh,
follow the frayed seam of my jeans,
shimmer, as the tree they peak through
stirs, wind being its master…
dribbles of warmth
leading nowhere,
just because—
       like baby kisses
       and promises.

Sunday

Sunday sneaks down
dragging a chain of faded, afternoon memories:
Dad snoring in his chair,
mouth open,
as though sleep overtook him mid-sentence,
his sock-covered feet
displaying holes where his work boots rubbed,
baseball hums on TV –
Red sox one, Yankees zip –
if I changed the channel, he'd wake, scold me,
Mom staring out the kitchen window
at her garden gone to weeds,
her limp cigarette gone to ash,
tiny bubbles crawling up the sides of
a glass of warm beer,
things left unsaid crouched
in dusty corners
needing a broom.

The Window

The window leaned against the tree
for three years, like a loyal friend refusing to go.
Rain gradually, relentlessly, coaxed paint
from the corners where the panes
met the wood. Not so you would
notice right away. You went by it
each day like clockwork, doing this
and that—you can't remember what right
now—and never noticed anything different. But,
then, one day, as your eyes followed a butterfly
drifting across the spring lawn visiting
newly-blossomed dandelions, they stopped
at the window, now enveloped by weeds, and
you said to yourself, 'Wow, it's peeling. How
long has it been there, anyway?'
No one was there to answer you, but, of course,
you knew the answer. It had been three years
since anyone had tugged you away from your
daily routine, or made you think about much of
anything at all.
Then the promise came back to you—the one
where he said he'd put that window where you
wanted it in the old garden shed you'd just
finished fixing up, hoping that would spur you
on to gardening projects that had languished
inside your head for ages. He'd set it there,
against the tree, along with a notation on his
daily calendar to put it in the old garden shed
where the broken one had fallen out.

But, as promises sometimes are, this one stood untouched. Somewhere, everything had stopped in mid-sentence and fell into a silent, airtight pocket, letting only weeds grow.

They Say

Forget what happened,
those things that bruised my soul,
forget, move on.
But truly,
who among us ever does
move on from yesterday;
isn't it always
there,
on top of your head,
dripping from your pen,
ruling your hand at the potter's wheel,
carving your face—
        always there,
        like cockroaches in the wall?
No matter which way you roll
at midnight,
or to what side
your pillow's turned,
yesterday's hurt walks
in your shoes—
        re-lived in every drop of rain
        that hits
        with impunity?

What

What is a person
a human being
is it a face
connecting tissues
muscles and bones and hair and feet and legs
blood – blood – blood
coursing through veins
and arteries, chambers of the heart
is it all of these
is it none
what makes us human
is it thoughts and ideas
is it mistakes or challenges we've
faced and overcome
is it anxieties we feel in the middle of he night
when the world we know is drenched in
darkness
is it forgiveness
or blame
or anger
or lust
or an undeniable weakness
in the pit of our stomachs
that tells us
everything we are is false
and nothing matters – nothing – nothing –
yes….

When It's Time

…who will take my shoes off,
whirl me round and round the
fragrant honeysuckle just
beyond the garden walls,
who will rub my aching feet
with tender calloused hands or
laugh through life's mysterious realm
while hiding in
our private pocket of eternity,
who will lie beside me listening to
my nonsense jokes
rippling the heavy air with laughter
meant for only me,
who will lift my ears up
off my morning pillow
with a dream-tale whisper
inviting me in,
who will kiss the years
from my eyes and
tug me back to my sixteenth summer
when everything in me was new?

…when the breeze no longer
lifts that curl of hair
just above your eye
leaving it for me to run my fingers through,
a bonfire I will build
then carry with me
those well-loved bones until…

Wild Thing
(Maurice Sendak, May, 2012)

Sendak's dead,
they said,
this man who
thumbed his nose at critics,
wrote what he saw,
wrote what
he felt—
fun and sorrow,
fear and silliness,
courage and love,
hovering on genius—
but who decides that?
So many rush in
tripping over their shoes
shouting 'I knew him,
he was this,
he was that'.
Inexplicably we
rush to judgment
after death
has taken our very best to
where they cannot
defend their lives
to anyone
but God.

Wonder

This world has ways
of dropping things on your head
things that
tear at your skin
smother your fragile body
and sometimes all you can do
is turn your head away
inhale from a different side of your mouth
look beyond
what or who is
doing the dropping
and tearing and
smothering wondering
can I go on living this way
yet you know
when the noise ends
when the wind melts to
a hushed whisper
when you are alone
with only your sob-choked breath
each heart
carries within its
beating thrusting pulsing walls
a choice to live - to live
or not.

Other books by Kathleen E. Fearing

Champ, 2010
An Old Heart, Yesterday and Today, 2010
Adisa's Basket, 2010
Women, Poems by Heart, 2011
My Friend the Werewolf, What Would You Do?
 2011
Voyage of Dreams, An Irish Memory, 2012

River quotations from:
www.thinkexist.com/quotes

Mornings by the River

15891074R00045

Made in the USA
Middletown, DE
26 November 2014